BUG ZOO

NICK BAKER

DK Publishing

DK

LONDON, NEW YORK,
MELBOURNE, MUNICH, and DELHI

Senior designer Sadie Thomas
Senior editor Ben Morgan
Designers Gabriela Rosecka, Lauren Rosier
Additional editing by Wendy Horobin
US editor Margaret Parrish
Photography Will Heap
Picture researcher Rob Nunn
Illustrations Laurie Peters
Production editor Clare McLean
Creative director Jane Bull
Category publisher Mary Ling

First published in the United States in 2010 by
DK Publishing, 375 Hudson Street
New York, New York 10014

A catalog record for this book
is available from the Library of Congress.
ISBN 978-0-7566-6166-3
Color reproduction by MDP, UK
Printed and bound by
Toppan, China

Discover more at
www.dk.com

WHO IS THIS?

2

CONTENTS

Do you know what I eat?

Welcome to Bug Zoo!!

Why start a bug zoo? Well, why not? Just because bugs are everywhere doesn't mean they're any less interesting than the animals you might see in a real zoo. In fact, the chances are that you know more about the exotic animals in a zoo than you do about the tiny creatures living right under your nose.

When I was growing up, my parents wouldn't let me keep animals in the house and I can't say I blame them. It didn't help my cause when my stick insects got out and defoliated my mom's houseplants or when I forgot to put the lid back on my ant city... But such mishaps didn't hold me back. We had an old shed and I quickly purloined it for my collection. Armed with a curious mind and a few jars, **I built my first bug zoo**, and, wow, did it open my eyes!

Each pot, pickle jar, and matchbox was a source of wonder, a dramatic little world with as much excitement as any TV soap opera. I witnessed what looked like scenes from a science fiction movie—some so terrifyingly bizarre they'd be unfit for broadcast. I saw MURDER and *cannibalism*, slashing blades, and chemical warfare. I watched caterpillars being reincarnated as butterflies. And I learned firsthand that **there's nothing ladylike about a ladybug!**

Starting a bug zoo is the perfect way to immerse yourself in the alien world of bugs. When you get down to their level (and that means getting *really* close—eye to compound eye, finger to feeler), it puts a fresh spin on the way you see things: a lawn becomes an exotic savanna, a hedge becomes a jungle, a backyard pond becomes as mysterious as the deep sea. You don't even need to use your imagination—there are unexplored worlds right on your doorstep, and the fantastical animals are real. You just have to open your eyes.

Building a zoo means you can become an explorer, a hunter, a collector of fine zoological specimens and, of course, a zookeeper. You don't need much to get started—just a table and a few jars will do. And you can capture your exhibits anywhere. Tune into their world and I can promise you this: you will never, ever be bored again.

Happy hunting!

Nick Baker

I proudly dedicate this book to my own little bug hunter, Elvie, whose very first word was "moth"!

Symbols

A few symbols appear throughout the book. This is what they mean:

 Where to find your bugs and how to capture them

 What to feed them and how to serve their meals

 Fun activities that reveal more about your bugs' natural behavior

 Humidity control and other tips to keep your bug house healthy

 Ask a parent for help when you see this warning symbol!

That's horrible!

 FEEDING TIME

ZOO TOOLS

All zookeepers need equipment to manage their collections, whether it's a broom and shovel to muck out the monkeys' cage or special tongs to move snakes around. The same applies to your bug zoo, so having the right gear on hand will make day-to-day bug maintenance just that little bit easier. The good news is that most of the things you need can be found around the house, so you won't need to raid the piggy bank.

Paper towel

I love this stuff and use it to carpet insect containers, to wipe up spilled gunk, to block vases (which stops insects from drowning), and to provide a source of moisture.

Paintbrush

Even the gentlest of fingers can squash a bug. For delicate jobs, a fine-haired paintbrush is essential. Use it to pick up pseudoscorpions, nudge caterpillars along, or even to brush out frass (insect poop) from awkward corners.

Notebook

It's a good idea to keep a notebook recording what goes on in the lives of your specimens. You can measure their growth and keep tabs on when they molt, mate, and feed. If you see any interesting behavior, jot it down—you may be the first person to witness it!

Tweezers (forceps)

These are a delicate extension of your own thumb and forefinger. While it's not a good idea to use them to handle bugs directly, they are useful for picking up other small items. You can make them more bug-friendly by gluing small foam pads to the ends!

Scissors

Useful for trimming paper towels and snipping sprigs off plants.

You can add sketches or photos to your notebook. Remember that many digital cameras have excellent "macro" lenses for taking close-ups.

Spoon

Ideal for scooping up everything from water creatures to ladybugs. When used in conjunction with a paintbrush, you have a miniature dustpan and brush!

You can make tweezers from wooden kebab skewers and a rubber band. Wind the band around one stick to form a hinge. Then wind the rest around both sticks.

Strainer or tea strainer

These are cheap and make excellent nets. The strainer is a great tool for pond dipping and can be taped to a plant stake for an instant pond net. The tea strainer is ideal for more delicate tasks, such as transferring creatures from tank to tank.

Mist sprayer

A regular spray with warm water will keep things nice and humid in your bug houses.

Labels

Make labels for your containers. Write down the type and number of bugs inside the container and the date you caught them.

Cardboard

Cardboard or black paper makes the perfect blind or privacy curtain.

Netting

Netting (or old pantyhose) can be used to make ventilation panels in insect cages, nets to capture bugs, or lids for jars, secured with a rubber band. Use **black netting** if you possibly can—it's much easier to see through.

Pencils

I prefer pencils to pens for making notes because if you spill water on your writing or it gets damp, you can still read it.

Magnifying lens

Probably one of the most useful pieces of gear any bug zoo owner can have. Most of the creatures in your collection are small, so anything that magnifies their lives will make studying them just that little bit more fun! Magnifications of 8x or 10x are perfect. Get the best one you can afford and keep it handy on a string around your neck.

Plastic lids

The lids of milk cartons and other containers make great food or water bowls.

Rubber bands

Useful for holding scraps of netting in place over the necks of jars.

USB microscope

Lets bring things up to date! These are not essential, but if you have a computer, a USB microscope will allow you to view small bugs in amazing detail. Most give you the option of recording still or moving images, and some magnify up to 200 times! A flexible stand helps give a steady image if you use high magnifications.

Glue

Craft glue or similar glue is useful for securing objects to the sides of containers and is not toxic to bugs that might unwittingly nibble it.

Tape

Masking tape is useful for sticking covers onto enclosures to create private and dark spaces for your captives.

CATCHING AND KEEPING

You don't need specialized containers for catching and keeping bugs. With a little trial and error, you'll soon discover how to adapt household containers for all your zoological needs, whether they're jars or boxes that once housed jelly, candy, chocolates, or shoes. The secret to creating a good habitat is to match the container to the animal and to make sure each type of bug gets just the right balance of moisture, ventilation, and temperature.

Making a pooter

It's a serious piece of gear with a silly name. A pooter is simply a suction device that allows you to collect very small creatures that would otherwise be frustratingly tricky to pick up. You can buy professional pooters but it's easy to make one out of common household items.

COLLECTING CAPTIVES

1. *Ask an adult to make two holes in the plastic lid of a spice or herb jar. An easy way to do this is to heat a metal skewer and use it to melt the plastic.*

2. *Cut two lengths of plastic tubing, 12 in (30 cm) and 8 in (20 cm) long. Push the ends of each through the holes in the plastic lid. They should fit snugly.*

Using the pooter

It's a good idea to practice with the pooter. Try sucking up grains of rice or rolled up balls of paper. Put the short tube in your mouth, position the end of the long tube over the dummy bug, and then give a short, sharp suck.

When trying it on live creatures, make sure you only use it on animals that will fit easily through the tube. Don't suck up slimy creatures or those with long legs or delicate wings that could get damaged. Oh, and one last tip: don't suck on the wrong tube, especially if you've already got insects in the pooter. It's not nice for you or them if you end up getting a mouthful of bugs!

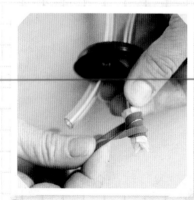

3. *Wrap cloth around the internal end of shorter tube and secure it with a rubber band. This is the tube you will suck through.*

4. *Put colored tape around the same tube. This is to remind you which tube to put in your mouth, which is critical, as you'll see later!*

The more you get into keeping and studying bugs, the more you'll become a connoisseur of containers!

Small plastic pots from deli tubs to glitter tubes are ideal for transporting bugs or housing small species. You can also buy specially made containers from biological suppliers.

Animal tanks from pet stores can serve as either aquariums or terrariums (dry habitats). Since small animals and moisture can escape through the slotted lid, you may need to put netting or a sheet of plastic under it.

Shoeboxes and plastic containers make good insect houses if you cut out a window and replace it with a see-through screen of black netting. See page 25.

Glass aquariums provide better visibility than plastic, since the glass does not scratch easily. See page 57 to find out how to create a freshwater habitat in an aquarium.

A homemade wormery is easy to make from wood, acrylic glass, and bulldog clips. Instructions on page 30.

Round tins can be adapted to make superb houses for larger insects. See page 48.

WOOD LICE

Go into your backyard now and lift something up—a rock, a log, a flowerpot, anything. It doesn't really matter, because you can bet that under each one will be a herd of what look like miniature armadillos: wood lice. Despite their familiarity, there is a lot more to wood lice than meets the eye, and they make a very interesting addition to your invertebrate zoo.

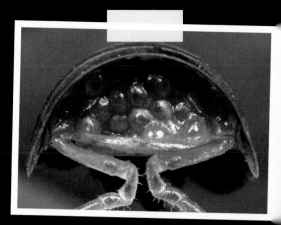

Brood pouch

The wood louse has a wonderful boat-shaped body, albeit an upside-down boat. Females use ample storage space to keep eggs in a fluid-filled "brood pouch." This usually contains about 50 eggs, but can hold as many as 260. The eggs ha a month or two after the adults mate and the youngsters then spend another week inside the pouch before being released.

CREATURE FEATURES

Exoskeleton

Wood lice must shed their external skeletons in order to grow. Unlike insects, they molt in two stages. First they take off their "pants" by molting the back half; then they molt the front half and go "topless." The old skin is eaten and recycled.

← Molted skin

Front half ready to molt

← New skin

ANTENNA

ARMOR PLATE

EYE

Legs

Count the legs. Wood lice have 14 and so are neither insects nor arachnids. They are actually crustaceans— close relatives of sea creatures like crabs and lobsters. While most crustaceans live in water, wood lice live on land but prefer damp places because they breathe through gills.

14 LEGS

Wood lice ha known to FOUR y

 Wood lice are known by many different names, including pill bugs, sow bugs, bibble bugs, doodlebugs, b

Close cousins

Wood lice belong to a branch of the crustacean family known as the isopods, the biggest of which are giant isopods up to 15 in (37 cm) long! These monsters are common in the sea. They trundle around on the seafloor scavenging on dead matter, just as wood lice do on land.

UNDERNEATH

Head

Thorax

Legs

Abdomen

Gills
Just like their aquatic relatives, wood lice breathe through gills. These need to be covered with a thin layer of water to work well, which is why wood lice need moisture. Some wood lice have developed lungs of sorts; these are seen as white patches on the gills. These white areas are riddled with air tubes that help the wood louse get oxygen from the air.

Uropods
Most wood lice have a pair of small tails called uropods. Aquatic crustaceans like lobsters have large uropods that they flap to help them swim. The small uropods of wood lice are used to produce defensive chemicals and to soak up water.

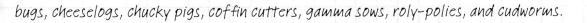

Pill bugs can roll into a ball for protection.

Who to keep

There are thousands of wood louse species, but you're most likely to find one of the five species below. Native to Europe, these have been spread by people and are now found worldwide.

Common rough wood louse
(*Porcellio scaber*)
The most common in my yard, it loves the drier places and is easily recognized by its gray matte appearance. Look at it through a magnifying glass and its surface is covered in tiny little pimples. Length ¾ in (17 mm).

Common shiny wood louse
(*Oniscus asellus*)
Probably the second most common species in yards, it looks glossy on the surface and has tiny yellowish flecks. Max. length ⅔ in (16 mm).

Pill bug
(*Armadillidium vulgare*)
This distinctive species has a smooth, glossy surface and an almost rounded or domed body. It's one of the few species that rolls into a ball when disturbed. Found in drier places than the others. Length ¾ in (18 mm).

Striped wood louse
(*Philoscia muscorum*)
This smaller species comes in a variety of different colors, from brick red to yellow as well as brown and gray, but one thing they all have is a dark stripe along the back. Length ⅜ in (11 mm).

Common pygmy wood louse
(*Trichoniscus pusillus*)
This pipsqueak reaches a top size of just under ¼ in (5 mm). It's actually common but often overlooked because of its size. The best place to find it is among leaf litter in woodlands. It has clusters of tiny little black eyes (three on each side) and the ends of its antennae are very fine and hairlike.

bugs, cheeselogs, chucky pigs, coffin cutters, gamma sows, roly-polies, and cudworms.

Use a plastic tub to collect your captives.

THE LOUSE HOUSE

Wood lice are easy to keep. The key to creating a good louse house is to understand their basic requirements: they like it dark and a little damp—but not soggy. A plastic or glass tank or jar with a little soil in is all that's needed, and because wood lice like to hide from view you need to provide a nice, dark **hiding place.**

To trap wood lice, bore a hole in a potato and put it in the backyard. Wood lice love dark, damp places and will soon crawl inside.

LOUSE ENCLOSURE

Black curtain

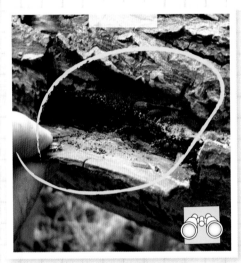

1. To find lots of wood lice, look under the bark of a rotten log or lift a rock and look underneath. If you go out at night with a flashlight you may find wood lice roaming around on walls, patios, and flowerbeds.

2. Put a layer of dirt or all-purpose potting soil in the bottom of the tank. As well as providing food, this will help control humidity. If you want, add some "furniture" to your louse house to make it look interesting.

3. Place a piece of bark against the side of the tank for the wood lice to hide behind. Prop it up with stones or glue it in place with silicone sealant.

4. To make the hiding place dark, tape a flap of cardboard on the outside of the tank to make a blackout curtain. Make sure you can lift it easily to spy on the wood lice.

To maintain a humid environment in your louse house, give the inside a couple of squirts with a mist sprayer each week and put a wad of damp moss in the tank.

Wood lice have a rotten diet, quite literally. They eat dead stuff, mainly plant material such as WOOD (hence their name), leaves, and the droppings of plant-eating animals. To add some variety, you can feed your wood lice pieces of **carrot and potato,** too.

Wood louse droppings may build up, but don't clean them out—the wood lice will EAT them. The droppings consist of dry, powdered wood that has passed through the wood louse's gut 90 percent undigested and so makes for another good meal! The droppings are also important in the recycling process, turning wood into soft pellets of compost that a host of other organisms can digest.

Dysdera

Wood lice produce defensive chemicals that make them taste foul to most predators, but a few specialized animals can eat them, including shrews, toads, and the so-called wood louse spiders (Dysdera).

Eeek, spider!!!

5. ADD YOUR CAPTIVES!

Bark

Potato

Tagging
One of the problems of dealing with animals that live in a colony is being able to identify and keep up with individuals. One solution is to use nontoxic permanent markers or paint to dab a very small colored spot on top of each wood louse. Make a record of who's who and note down what they get up to each day. Remember, though, that when a wood louse sheds its skin it will shed its mark and its identity!

6. After a day or so, the wood lice will have settled in and found the hiding place. Lift the blackout curtain to watch them, but don't keep it open too long or they'll see through your scheme and wander off looking for another dark place to hide.

SLUGS & SNAILS

Slugs and snails are almost universally hated by human beings thanks to the habits of the relatively few species that have a taste for garden plants. However, if you get to know these creatures well you'll discover a secret world that—although a little slimy— is filled with fascinating weirdness and surprisingly little to loathe.

Slugs are essentially snails without shells. Having no shell means they can slip into tiny gaps and squirm into soil, but they are more prone to drying out.

Hairy snails

Mantle

CREATURE FEATURES

Distant cousin!

Meet the family

Slugs and snails belong to a huge family of animals known as mollusks. The mollusks mostly live in water and include octopuses, squid, and all the creatures that live inside seashells. The shell dwellers come in two forms: those with a shell made of two halves, like clams, and those with a classic seaside seashell—the gastropods. Slugs and snails are gastropods, too. The word gastropod means "belly foot," and if you watch how a snail "walks" you'll realize it's a truly excellent name.

SHELL

Most snail shells are "right-handed," meaning that the spiral curls clockwise (to the right) from the center. But if you're lucky you might find a left-handed snail. These are very rare and are known as "snail kings."

THE TAIL

This is not really a true tail but the trailing edge of the foot.

slug's breathing hole

Mites!

The world's **largest** land snail is the giant African snail. One specimen grew to 15 in (39.3 cm) when fully extended!

BREATHING HOLE

Slugs and snails breathe through a hole in the mantle. Look very closely at a slug's breathing hole and you might notice excitable white specks running in and out. These are mites that live on the slug's skin.

Growth ridges

A snail's shell is made of the mineral calcium carbonate (chalk), which snails get from their food. Look carefully at a shell and you'll see tiny ridges. These are growth rings that develop as growth slows down in winter and then speeds up again in spring.

Chalk

Use a flashlight to watch the eye shoot down the tentacle!

MANTLE

The materials that form a snail's shell are produced by a special part of the body wall called the mantle. When a snail retreats into its shell, it's the mantle you're left looking at. In slugs, the mantle is the thickened, leathery area on their back.

EYES

At the tips of the long tentacles are tiny eyes like black dots. These sense light and dark and can't see much else. Touch a snail's eye with your finger—it will shoot down the tentacle as the tentacle rolls in on itself like a pullover sleeve. Wait a moment and the tentacle will come back out as blood is pumped into it.

SHELL LIP

If the edge of the shell is thin and papery, the snail is still growing. If there's a nice, thick lip, the snail is fully grown.

TENTACLES

The four wiggly tentacles on the front are the snail's main sense organs. The long top pair contain eyes. The lower pair are sensitive to touch, taste, and smell.

very sensitive

MOUTH

Slugs and snails scrape at leaves with a special kind of tongue called a radula, which is covered with tiny teeth.

THE FOOT

This is not a foot in the classic sense, but a very muscular organ used to "surf" the carpet of slime the snail lays down as it moves.

FOOT FRINGE

Eye

MAKE A MOLLUSK MANSION

For tiny snail species, any clear-sided container is fine, but for larger species such as common garden snails, use a big jar or an old fish tank. Your snail house must have a SECURE LID that the snails can't push off. You'll also need to maintain a humid environment, but with enough ventilation to stop things from getting moldy and smelly.

Finding your captives

Go out on a warm, wet night and you'll find slugs and snails everywhere, but during the day nothing but a **silvery trail** can be seen. This is because these animals have thin skin and **lose water** easily in bright sun or wind. When the sun goes down, the humidity rises and they come out of hiding. To find them during the day, look under rocks and flowerpots, behind ivy, or in dark, damp crevices.

Maintenance of your "Gastropets" palace

Feeding

You'll soon realize how fussy slugs and snails can be—not all of them like our lettuces, despite what gardeners may think! Give your animals a choice and experiment with their diet. Try cucumber, tomatoes, bread, wild plants, dead leaves, grass clippings, and dead wood. Put the food in small dishes to keep things neat.

Climate control

If your snails stop moving, they may be too dry. In dry weather, snails can go into a form of hibernation known as "estivation" and may even seal their shells shut with a waterproof skin. To keep humidity up, spray them with a little water once a day and reduce ventilation so the moisture doesn't evaporate too quickly.

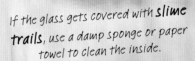

SNAIL ENCLOSURE

Don't forget to provide a secure lid.

If the glass gets covered with slime trails, use a damp sponge or paper towel to clean the inside.

Dead wood

Place soil in the bottom.

What do a great white shark and a garden snail have in common?

Look for glass snails, which have transparent shells.

Tagging
To keep track of individuals, mark their shells with a permanent marker or dots of nail polish. You can do the same with the snails in your yard. For instance, mark those behind the shed 1 to 10 in red and those under the ivy 1 to 10 in yellow. Then go out at night with a flashlight and plot their positions on a map of your yard. How far do they wander? Do they return home?

Old timer
The owner of the snail above colored it with purple nail polish one year and pink the next and discovered that it stayed in the same yard for years.

Radula

Reveal the radula
To see your snail's mouth in action, make a soupy mixture from honey, water, and ground-up leaves and paint this on the inside of your mollusk house. Then wait for one of your mollusks to discover the treat (or place a snail on the glass). From outside you'll see the special tongue, or "radula," in action as your snail scrapes off the sugary mixture to satisfy its several thousand sweet teeth!

Banded snail

Mmm, I smell fresh bread!

The smell test
Once you've discovered your snails' favorite food, why not **test their powers of smell?** First, give your snails an appetite by starving them for a couple of days. (Don't feel bad, in France they do this before cooking them—at least yours will have a happier ending.) Put the snails on a smooth table, place the food nearby, and watch. Move the food and see if the snails follow it. What's the maximum distance over which they respond?

It's said that a garden snail can smell food from 20 in (50 cm) away!

Snails need a source of calcium for their shells. This is easy to supply in the form of a cuttlefish bone, which you can buy in a pet store.

Teeth! Like a shark, a snail has rows of teeth that keep getting replaced so they don't get blunt.

APHIDS... THE HUNGRY HERDS

Meet the family

There are around 4,500 aphid species, of which the most familiar are those that wash out of our salad: greenflies and blackflies (although neither is a true fly and for most of the year they don't even have wings). The rest of the family come in all kinds of colors, including pink, yellow, gray, mottled, and white. All of them feed by poking their mouthparts into plants and drinking the sap that flows out.

Also known as greenflies, aphids are plant-eating pests hated by gardeners the world over. I've included them in the book not only because they make great food for other species in your bug zoo, especially ladybugs, but also because aphids are actually fascinating little animals in their own right. With a little help from a magnifying glass or microscope, you'll discover some of the weird tricks that make these little insects have such a BIG impact.

In perfect conditions, a single aphid can produce a family of BILLIONS in a single year!

CREATURE FEATURES

CORNICLES
The pair of strange, pointed things sticking out backward from the aphid's behind are called cornicles. They are used in defense and produce an oily secretion called cornicle wax. Ladybugs hate it.

WINGS
In good conditions, aphids are wingless. But if food runs out, the weather turns bad, or a colony gets crowded, females give birth to babies that will develop wings. Called "alates," their job is to fly off and find greener pastures—or at least a juicier rose bush!

ANTENNA

THORAX

HEAD

EYE

ABDOMEN

LEGS (6)

STYLETS
Aphids have piercing mouthparts called stylets that they push into plants to drink a sugary liquid called sap.

CAUDA
This is the tail-like spike that sticks out of an aphid's rear. Some species use this in defense or to flick away droplets of honeydew (aphid poop).

Finding aphids

In spring and summer you'll find aphids on the leaves and stalks of sweet peas, beans, roses, thistles, stinging nettles, and maple trees. If you don't have these plants in your yard, plant fava beans or sweet peas in spring and the aphids will soon appear.

HOUSING THE HERD

You don't really need a "house" for your herd. All you need to keep aphids is a plant infested with them and a jar of water or vase. Use scissors to take a cutting and transfer it carefully to the jar. I say "carefully" because if you jolt the stem, the insects will drop off, thinking they're under attack by a giant predator. Keep the aphid jar in a sunny place—a windowsill is ideal.

Place the aphid jar on a black mat or black paper to collect molted skins and droplets of sticky honeydew.

MAINTAINING THE HERD

As your aphids multiply, they will take their toll on the plant they're all sucking on. To make sure they get enough food, add fresh cuttings to the jar. Aphids can be fussy feeders, so always use the same type of plant. Make sure the fresh stem touches the old one near the clusters of aphids so that the aphids will find it and move across.

Sweet pea plant

Aphids

Keep the plant watered

Thinning out

You may need to thin out the numbers if things get crowded—otherwise the colony will start producing winged females that fly off to find new plants. Use a small paintbrush to tap unwanted aphids into a container. You can feed these to your ladybugs or release them back into the yard—an act that will probably mystify your parents!

Yum, dinner!

19

THE APHID'S SECRET WEAPON

Use a paintbrush to knock off every aphid except one.

Here's an experiment that will show you just why aphids are so successful. Simply take a cut stem with a few aphids on it and knock off all but the biggest and fattest one without wings. This is your foundress and she will be a female (they almost always are). Your job now is to make a note of the date and, each day, record the number of aphids on the plant. It won't be long before lots of babies appear...

Week 1

Week 2

Week 3

A female aphid lives about a month and has 3–8 babies a day. Now, in some species each of these is born *already pregnant* and can start giving birth a week later. In this way, a single female can give rise to billions of aphids in a year. If all the offspring of your foundress survived and gave birth themselves, you'd have enough insects after a year to make a line stretching more than four times around the Earth. That would require a lot of sweet peas! Fortunately, this never happens, since aphids are eaten by many other animals.

Virgin birth

The aphid's secret weapon is the ability to give birth without mating, a trick known as parthenogenesis. Quite a few insects do this and it lets them exploit a food supply quickly. To speed things up even more, aphids give birth to live young rather than laying eggs, and, as we've seen, those babies are born pregnant—something scientists call "telescoping generations." It's a little like Russian dolls, but with living insects.

What do bees use to make "forest honey"?

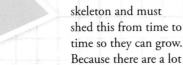
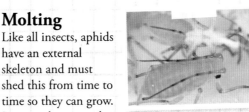

Molting

Like all insects, aphids have an external skeleton and must shed this from time to time so they can grow. Because there are a lot of aphids in your colony, there will nearly always be someone molting. Watch how they split open their old skin and almost drop out upside down. Put a piece of black paper under the colony and watch the empty skins pile up.

Do aphids have a sense of smell?

Wings

Toward the end of the year, winged females and males appear. These mate and then disperse, the females either hibernating or laying eggs. Winged females may appear at other times if the colony gets overcrowded.

Watch how an aphid responds when you touch it gently but repeatedly with a fine-haired paintbrush. You might see a fluid come out of the ends of its cornicles. This waxy secretion is sticky and in some species contains foul-tasting chemicals and a scent known as an alarm pheromone. The scent warns other members of the herd that they're under attack.

> Aphids plug their sharp stylets into a plant's veins and then sit back as the plant's sugary food supply is pumped right through their bodies. They don't even have to suck!

> Quick, run!

Watch what happens if you get some of the waxy secretion on your paintbrush and waft it around. The other aphids will pull out their stylets and **drop off the plant** or move quickly away from the source of the smell and trouble. Take the paintbrush to an undisturbed colony of aphids and see how close it needs to be before they smell the pheromone and react.

Honeydew poop

Look closely at your herd and you might see droplets of shiny liquid oozing out of the aphids' tails. This is aphid poop and it's called honeydew. Aphids feed by tapping into a plant's plumbing system to steal a sugary liquid called sap, which is made in leaves and carried around the plant in veins. The sap is full of sugar but has little protein, so aphids must swallow a great deal of it to get all the nutrients they need. The excess sugar and water pass out of the other end as sticky honeydew.

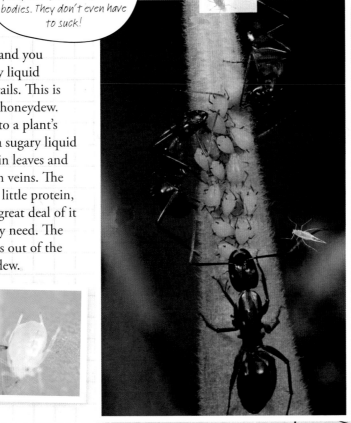

Husks

Some of your aphids may stop moving and change color. Look closer—you may find that the body is just an empty husk with a tiny hole in its abdomen. This "mummy" is all that's left after a parasitic grub laid by a wasp has eaten the aphid's insides, before turning into an adult wasp and escaping through the hole. It can't be a nice way to die!

Ant farmers

Some species of ants "farm" aphids to collect honeydew. The ants protect the aphids from predators and even move them around on the plant if food is drying up. In return, the aphids let the ants "milk" them like herds of cattle.

Aphid poop (honeydew)! It's a delicious and highly prized honey in many parts of the world.

21

CATERPILLARS

Caterpillars turn into butterflies or moths, this we know; but how do they actually get there? The magical transformation is one of nature's great miracles, and it's also something that anybody—given a few pieces of basic information—can witness firsthand by rearing caterpillars at home. All you have to do is find a few caterpillars (most species will do) and keep them well fed. But be warned: caterpillars are hungry animals!

CREATURE FEATURES

SETAE
Caterpillars have lots of sensory hairs called setae that detect objects and vibrations.

ABDOMEN

Life cycle
The life cycle of butterflies involves what we call "complete metamorphosis," which means the adult and juvenile stages are totally different. Insects that undergo complete metamorphosis actually have four stages in their life cycles: **egg**, **larva**, **pupa**, and **adult**.

LIFE CYCLE

Egg

Larva (caterpillar)

Pupa (chrysalis)

Adult (butterfly)

Red admiral butterfly

Hatching
Caterpillars are really just food-processing units, their job being simply to eat and grow. After hatching, tiny new caterpillars are only a few millimeters long and usually have to eat their own egg (some species die if they don't). Once they've nibbled their way out, the feasting begins in earnest...

Between hatching and their final molt, caterpillars balloon in weight. Hawkmoth caterpillars multiply in weight 10,000 times in only 20 days! Although their bodies are soft, caterpillars do have exoskeletons (albeit ones that stretch) that limit growth. As a result, they must molt 4–5 times as they grow. The final molt reveals a chrysalis or pupa, and it is inside this that the last and most miraculous change takes place.

Owl butterfly caterpillar

TUBERCLE

Many caterpillars have wartlike bumps called tubercles. The tubercles often have spines or hairs that are sometimes (but not always) poisonous or able to sting.

Tussah silk moth caterpillar

THORAX

ANTENNA

HEAD

TRUE LEGS

Count the legs. You might find as many as 16, but caterpillars are insects and insects should only have six! So what's going on? Well, at the front of the body are the six "true legs," which look like normal insect legs and have joints.

FALSE LEGS

The five pairs of legs behind the true legs are called false legs or prolegs. These remind me of jelly-bean limbs, all short and squishy. Each ends in a fringe of tiny velcrolike hooks called crochets.

SPIRACLES

Look carefully along the side of a caterpillar and you'll see breathing holes, or spiracles, on each segment. These let air into breathing tubes that run throughout the body.

EYES

There are clusters of very simple eyes called ocelli on either side of the head. They can't "see" well but can tell the difference between light and dark.

MANDIBLE (JAW)

MOUTHPARTS

Caterpillars have jaws called mandibles that work side to side to slice up leaves. Under these are the maxillae, a pair of smaller jaws that taste food and make sure it's up to standard.

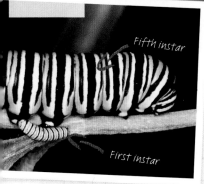

Fifth instar

First instar

Monarch caterpillar

Monarch caterpillars take only two weeks to reach full size, molting four times along the way. The different stages between molts are known as "instars."

THE "PILLA VILLA"

In the wild, caterpillars live in a salad bowl and never have to move far for their next mouthful, which is something to keep in mind when you rear them in captivity. In addition to providing plenty of fresh food, you'll need to prevent your pilla villa from becoming stale or too humid, which can encourage bacteria and fungi—two of the caterpillar farmer's biggest enemies.

The easy way to get caterpillars is to buy them by mail order! There are lots of butterfly suppliers who will mail eggs, caterpillars, or pupae to you. It's cheating, but it's a good way to obtain exotic species that you'd never find at home.

Finding caterpillars

You can find caterpillars by searching the undersides of leaves on plants and bushes in the spring and summer. Another technique is to do a little "bush beating." Place a white sheet or upturned umbrella under a branch and wack the plant hard with a stick. Any insects, including caterpillars, will drop off. But the best way to collect caterpillars is to watch out for female butterflies laying eggs and then collect these. This way, you'll know exactly what species you've got.

Use a paintbrush to nudge your caterpillars if you need to move them.

BUILDING AN ENCLOSURE

As they grow, caterpillars will need larger containers. For eggs and tiny caterpillars I use small plastic boxes lined with paper towels. These can get sweaty from condensation, so to improve ventilation, cut a hole out of the lid, stretch netting across, and clip the lid back on. Larger caterpillars need taller containers that can house plants in a vase or jar of water. A varnished cardboard box (right) works well. Alternatively, make a cylindrical insect house from a cookie tin (see page 48).

1. *To make a caterpillar house from a cardboard box, start by cutting a window in one side. If you're using a shoe box, cut a window in the lid. The window will go at the front.*

2. *Waterproof the inside and outside of the box with a coat of quick-drying varnish. This stops it from getting damp and falling apart.*

A plastic tub makes a good home for smallish caterpillars.

3. *Line the window with fine netting from a fabric store or an old pair of pantyhose. Black netting is best since it's easy to see through. If you don't have a shoe box, make a cardboard frame to hold the netting in place.*

4. *Line the floor with tissue paper and put in a suitable plant. The leaves must touch the sides of the box so wandering caterpillars can find them. Plug the vase or jar with modeling clay to stop the caterpillars from drowning.*

Feeding

Your caterpillars will need a regular supply of the right kind of plant. To replace the chewed old plant material, put fresh new stems in with it and then wait an hour or so for the caterpillars to walk onto the new stuff. Then carefully remove the old plant. Any stray caterpillars can be gently lifted across, but if they're about to molt (see right), don't touch them! Instead, keep the piece of stem they're on.

Fresh food

Tussah silk moth caterpillar

I'll have the next size up please!

If a caterpillar isn't moving or looks under the weather, it may be about to molt. There may be a bulge behind the head, and if you touch the caterpillar it may simply move from side to side rather than flee. Moving your caterpillar at this point may damage or even kill it, so leave it in place and keep an eye on it. When they're about to molt, most caterpillars spin a little silk pad that's difficult to see (unless it's on the side of the container). The caterpillar then hooks its rear feet to this silk. A Y-shaped split opens up on the head capsule, and the "new" caterpillar, in a fresh and bigger skin, crawls out, leaving the old skin attached to the silk pad. After a little rest, while it waits for its new, soft skin to harden, the caterpillar returns to doing what it does best: stuffing its face.

Emperor moth caterpillar (5th instar)

Molted skin

Mucking out
Caterpillars, being eating machines, make a lot of droppings (the technical word for which is frass). Your caterpillar house will need mucking out every day at least to keep things clean and prevent disease. Throw away the paper towel and frass, wipe down the inside of the box, and then line it again with a new paper towel. Easy!

Frass

A caterpillar has around 4,000 muscles in its body, of which more than 200 are in its head. A human has at most 850!

CHRYSALISES

When your caterpillars have gotten so big they can't stuff another leaf past their mandibles, something odd happens. Butterfly caterpillars no longer have a taste for their food, stop moving, and may hang from a leaf or lasso themselves to a stem. Moth caterpillars may start racing around their cage, trying to find some soil in which to bury themselves, or may enclose themselves in a cocoon of silk or leaves.

The caterpillars are getting ready for the next change and will soon shed the last of their skins to reveal something totally different: a **chrysalis** (in butterflies) or a **pupa** (in moths). Keep checking your caterpillar when it's ready to start this process, since it's definitely worth watching. If you haven't identified the species, give it plenty of options: put some twigs, some bark, and a good 2–3 in (5–8 cm) of soil in its cage.

Small tortoiseshell caterpillar

Swallowtail butterfly

MAKE A CHRYSALIS TREE

Life goes on beneath the chrysalis skin, but other than an occasional wiggle or squeak, there's little activity. This stage can last a few weeks or, if the chrysalises form in the fall, probably a whole winter. Butterfly chrysalises should remain on their twigs, but you can snip off the twigs and pin them to a board or a more robust branch if you want. Make sure the emerging butterflies will have room to perch and stretch their wings. If necessary, you can remove chrysalises from their silk pads and reattach them to a new support with cotton (below).

1.

A chrysalis that has attached itself to a container is best left in place, but if you have move it, tease it gently away from the silk pad.

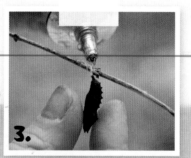

2.

Pull the cremaster (tail) through some cotton balls so that the tiny hooks catch threads of cotton.

Swallowtail caterpillars attach their rear ends to a pad of silk on a stem and then spin what looks like a seatbelt to hold themselves in place.

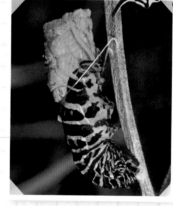

The skin splits behind the head, and what bulges out is not very caterpillar-like at all! The chrysalis is soft and flexible and wriggles to push the old skin backward.

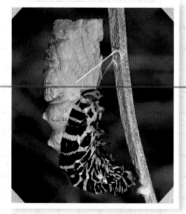

The skin wrinkles like a sock. When it gets to the end, the chrysalis unhooks its tail, flicks aside the skin, and reattaches to the silk pad with a velcrolike tip called a cremaster.

The real magic now begins. Inside the chrysalis, the cells of the caterpillar break down into a kind of living soup and then reorganize themselves into a completely new body form: a butterfly.

3.

Glue the cotton to a twig using a tiny dab of superglue so that the chrysalis hangs naturally. Make sure there is room for the emerging butterfly.

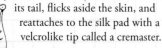

26

Ta-daa!

Keep a close eye on your chrysalises when they look ready to open. The chrysalis skin, now thin and brittle, will split at the head first as the butterfly begins to push its way out.

Small tortoiseshell chrysalis

You can tell when a butterfly is about to emerge because the skin of the pupa or chrysalis changes color dramatically. In moths it usually darkens and softens at the same time, while in butterflies it becomes transparent. You can sometimes get a sneak preview of the colors of the adult's wings through the skin.

Within minutes the butterfly will wriggle out and perch on the old skin. Its body is very soft, fragile, and damp at this stage so don't touch it.

The wings at first are crumpled and wet, but as the insect pumps fluid into the wing veins, they will expand. After a couple of hours, the wings will have dried and hardened and the butterfly will have completed its preflight checks. It will now be ready for release back into the wild.

Elephant hawkmoth

Keeping moth pupae

Many moth caterpillars bury themselves in the ground to pupate. If you have moth caterpillars that turn into pupae on the floor of your caterpillar house, lay them on sterile potting soil or a bed of moss and keep them somewhere cool and dark (a shed is perfect), preferably out of reach of mice, which love to snack on these immobile packages of protein.

Elephant hawkmoth pupa

Don't be alarmed if your new butterfly seems to be leaking blood! This fluid, called meconium, is left over after the wings are pumped up and is natural.

Small tortoiseshell adult

WORMS

The earthworm is one of the simplest animals you can keep in a bug zoo. It has no eyes, no ears, no legs, no face, and no limbs of any kind. Yet this lowly creature has more ecological importance than anything else in this book, and for that reason alone it's worth including in your collection. Worms are very easy to keep. The biggest problem is actually seeing what they're up to because worms, being worms, will do what they're good at—and that's burrowing! But even if you don't get to see much of your exhibits, you can still find out why these natural recyclers are so good at improving soil.

Record breakers
There are giant earthworm species that can grow to 13 ft (4 m) in length, such as the Gripsland earthworm of Australia and the Mekong giant earthworm of Asia.

SKIN
The skin of a worm is its eyes, ears, nose, and tongue all in one. Every square millimeter has more than 700 taste receptors, making worms very sensitive to what's going on around them. Worms can't see, but they do have many light-sensitive cells on the surface of their skin.

CREATURE FEATURES

ANUS

TAIL END
The tail end is usually flatter and almost paddle shaped and can be expanded to wedge a worm into its hole. Many species reach out of their burrows on warm, wet nights, keeping their tail in the burrow like an anchor, and at the slightest disturbance they can withdraw by tightening up their muscles.

SETAE
Each segment has four pairs of small, stiff bristles called "setae," used to grip the walls of burrows (handy when a bird is tugging at the other end). You can feel them if you pull a worm gently through your fingers. Put a worm on dry paper and the setae make a scratchy sound.

Is the worm above male or female?

HEAD END

All the vital organs are in the front section between the mouth and the saddle. In here are the worm's five hearts, its brain, its stomach, and the reproductive parts. While it's not true that cutting a worm in half will give you two worms, the front section can survive and grow a new tail.

SADDLE

The saddle is the most obvious feature on an adult worm. This thickened organ produces a slimy glue that holds worms together when they mate. When a worm lays eggs, the saddle slides off to form a capsule around them.

SEGMENTS

MOUTH

Brandling worm
(*Eisenia fetida*)
One of the easiest species to find is the brandling worm, also known as the tiger worm because of its distinctive striped appearance. When threatened, it produces a yellow fluid that smells bad, which is possibly why it's also known as the garlic worm. Brandling worms are found in heaps of rotting plant material, especially compost heaps.

Night crawler
(*Lumbricus terrestris*)
This is one of the biggest of the garden worm species and can reach 1 ft (30 cm) long. Night crawlers hide in deep burrows during the day, but you can find them on lawns on warm, wet nights when they come up to find fresh food. Step carefully if you look for them—they are incredibly shy and quickly dart back underground.

Black head
(*Aporrectodea longa*)
This is the species responsible for making worm casts on your lawn. These squiggly heaps of what looks like fine soil are little piles of worm poop! Black heads are handsome worms with a dark gray head end, and they make good guests in a wormery. You might even get to watch them make their casts.

Worm hunting
You can find worms under rocks and flowerpots at any time, but the best time to hunt them is on damp summer nights, when the really big worms come out of the ground to search for fresh food. Earthworms can't see the color red, so a flashlight covered with a red filter makes a handy hunting tool. To find brandling worms, rummage through a compost container.

MAKING A WORMERY

A wormery can be as simple as a large jar (giant pickle jars work well) or a plastic tub. What you put in your wormery depends on what type of worm you've got: brandling worms prefer rotting plant material; other types of worms need some soil.

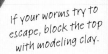

The deluxe wormery

The only problem with using a jar as a wormery is that your worms can hide in the middle where you won't see them. The deluxe wormery allows you to view your captives much more frequently. You don't need to be good at carpentry to make the one shown here, since it's very simple. All it requires is a strip of wood (the thinner the better), a sheet of acrylic glass, and four big bulldog clips.

Feeding
Leaf litter, potato peel, and grass clippings all make good worm food. Leave them on the surface and the worms will do the rest. Keep in mind a worm can eat more than half its body weight in food in a day—so they'll need lots of food!

If your worms try to escape, block the top with modeling clay.

Add Worms

WORM ENCLOSURE

1. Ask an adult to cut the acrylic into squares about 12 in (30 cm) wide and to cut the wood into three lengths to form a frame that fits the acrylic squares.

2. Place the other acrylic square on top to sandwich the wooden frame between the two clear sheets.

3. Clip the corners to hold everything together. Presto! You have now built a wormery. If the bulldog clips are large enough, the wormery should stand up on its own.

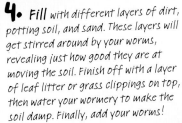

4. Fill with different layers of dirt, potting soil, and sand. These layers will get stirred around by your worms, revealing just how good they are at moving the soil. Finish off with a layer of leaf litter or grass clippings on top, then water your wormery to make the soil damp. Finally, add your worms!

5. Make a black curtain from cardboard or cover the wormery with light-proof cloth. This keeps the soil dark and the worms won't be shy of wriggling next to the acrylic glass, where you can see them.

Digging machines

An acre of pasture contains up to 3 million worms that dig about 9 miles (15 km) of tunnels a day! You can watch these digging machines in action inside your wormery. They move by using muscles to squeeze fluid into different parts of the body. First, fluid is pumped into the streamlined head end to make it stretch out into the soil. Next, more fluid is pumped in to make the head expand and force the soil apart.

Worm

 Poop factory

Worms do a great job of improving soil. In addition to stirring it up with all their digging, they recycle dead matter by eating it and turning it into worm poop—the perfect compost for plants! You can manufacture worm compost by making a wormery from plastic boxes. This kind of wormery works best with brandling worms (*Eisenia fetida*). They love all kinds of dead plant material from rotten fruit and potato peelings to soggy leaves.

1. Ask an adult to cut a hole in the bottom of a plastic box, leaving a wide frame around the hole.

2. Place wire mesh in the bottom of the box over the hole. Worm poop will fall through the mesh.

3. Stack your box in an empty one with space below to collect compost.

4. Fill the top box with peelings or leaves (not soil), and add your worms. Make ventilation holes or a netting window in the lid and put the lid on.

Worm poop

Old carrot peelings

THINGS TO LOOK FOR

Eggs and babies

If you pick through your poop factory carefully, you might notice worm eggs. These are tiny little almost lemon-shaped cocoons. If you hold them up to the light and examine them with a magnifying glass, you might be able to see the brand new brandlings inside. When your wormery is established, you'll also find dozens of baby worms squirming in the gunk.

Baby worm

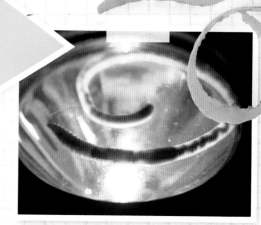

 See-through worm

Put a worm on a flashlight and examine it with a hand lens for a look inside the worm's body! You'll see the worm's squiggly gut as a dark silhouette, with a bright red blood vessel running along it. Watch the blood vessel pulse as blood pulses along it. You might be able to see the five hearts causing this blood rush—they will show up as thickened red blotches toward the head. Lots of small white tubes called nephridia (which work like kidneys) may be visible, as well as two pairs of white calcium sacks, which are thought to be involved with digestion and maybe reproduction.

Moisture

A worm's body is 75–90 percent water, and for this reason it's important that you don't let your wormery dry out. Keep the soil damp but not soggy. Waterlogged soil contains very little oxygen and will cause the worms to suffocate or drown.

EARWIGS

These shy creatures are common enough and are usually seen scuttling for cover when disturbed. They are instantly recognizable thanks to that most distinctive of features: the "pincers" that protrude from their rear ends. But what else do you know about earwigs? Earwigs have a PR problem because people think they crawl inside your ear and eat your brain—not true. They're not even that much of a pest in the garden. Get to know them and you'll find they make great little additions to your bug zoo.

CREATURE FEATURES

ANTENNA

EYE

HEAD

MOUTH

PALP

THORAX

Earwigs are flattened in profile, allowing them to squeeze easily under and between things. They love hiding in tight crevices and can often be found lurking under rocks.

Why are they called "earwigs"?

Some say it's because the flying wings look ear shaped when unfolded, giving you "earwing"—a nice idea, but unlikely, since these are rarely seen. Others suggest it's because the pincers look a little like ear-piercing tools. Many of the names given to them in other countries back this up, for example, *perce-oreille* (ear piercer) in French. They were called *earwicga* in old English, and *ohrwurm* in German— which mean "ear creature" and "ear worm" respectively. These names are probably a reference to them crawling into tight, dark places, such as inside ears, which probably happened quite often when people used to sleep on mattresses stuffed with hay.

Grrr...

Bamboo canes can be used to make an earwiggery—turn the page to see how. Earwigs often hide in these in the yard.

WINGS

The wings are hidden under wing covers, or elytra. Earwigs can fly, but their wings are folded so intricately (40 times) that it takes ages to unpack them.

There are 1,900 species of earwig in the world, but the common earwig (*Forficula auricularia*) is the one you see most often. Originally from Europe, it is now found on every continent except Antarctica.

LEGS (6)

PINCERS

Earwigs use their pincers, or "cerci," for a multitude of tasks, including defense (they threaten and try to nip but cannot generate enough force to hurt), unfolding the very complex wings, subduing struggling prey, and (probably) breeding.

Mr. and Mrs. Earwig can be told apart by the size and shape of their pincers. Males have large, very curved ones, while the females have narrower and straighter ones.

ABDOMEN

The male has 10 visible segments, while females have only eight.

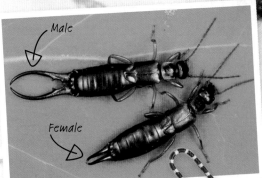

Male

Female

33

MAKING AN EARWIGGERY

Earwigs are "thigmotaxic," which means they can't stand open spaces and don't relax unless their bodies are pressed tightly against a surface. They are also nocturnal. So the challenge to a bug zookeeper is to keep these animals happy and behaving naturally in captivity, while also being able to see what they're getting up to. For that reason, a little bit of thought and effort needs to be given to the construction of your "earwiggery."

Catching an earwig

Earwigs are not hard to find, but they move fast when discovered! They like to hide in dry, dark places but some locations are earwiggier than others. Look under logs (particularly any with loose bark) piles of bricks, plant pots, and even inside dead hollow plant stems. In the winter you can often find hibernating earwigs by splitting the stems lengthwise. There may be other insects hiding there, too.

You can trap earwigs with a flowerpot. Block the hole in the bottom and fill with straw. Dribble a little honey onto the straw and upend the whole thing onto a short garden cane. Place it near the compost heap or among the flowerbeds. After a week, several earwigs will have taken up residence in your trap.

Alternatively, stack sheets of cardboard on a garden cane and use this to stake them to the ground so they don't blow away. Many insects, including earwigs, will move into this high-rise bug hotel.

EARWIG ENCLOSURE

1. Collect some hollow stems or canes. Get an adult to split them in half for you. Scrape out any pith, then glue them to the lid or sides of a clear box using water-based or craft glue.

Use an old chocolate box

2. Spread a little damp soil, moss, or leaf litter over the base of your container. This will keep the atmosphere humid, but don't add too much or the earwigs will burrow into it and you won't be able to watch them.

3. Add your earwigs, then replace the lid. Cover the lid with cardboard to make it dark. The earwigs will squeeze into the pieces of split cane, allowing you to peel back the curtain and find them!

Snug as a bug in a rug!

Little is known about earwigs, so anything you witness in your earwig enclosure is worth recording. I've never seen them mate, but apparently the females choose the males with the biggest pincers. After mating, the female excavates a burrow for her eggs. She lays 30–50 eggs and tends them vigilantly, often licking them or moving them around the burrow. When they hatch she continues to brood them, bringing the babies food until they're old enough to leave the nest.

Feeding

Earwigs have a wide range of tastes and will eat many things, both living and dead. Their favorite place for dining out is a compost heap. Here they can find other small creatures and their eggs and larvae, as well as lots of rotting plant material, algae, and fungi. Try experimenting with your earwigs' menu to see what they prefer.

Cucumber

Water is very
important to earwigs, so it helps to keep the atmosphere humid—not so wet that everything becomes moldy, but not bone dry either. Add a small dish of water-soaked cotton balls, moss, or paper towels to make sure they don't get thirsty.

LADYBUGS

I find it hard to resist correcting people when I hear them talking about ladybugs as cute little beetles. Sure they're good for the garden, and yes the majority of them (not all) have bright and perky colors. But these predators are not as ladylike or as gentle as we've been led to think. Watching a ladybug mow its way through a herd of greenfly is like watching a horror film, with pieces of greenfly flying everywhere, and plenty of blood and gore, too. You have been warned. Keeping ladybugs is not for the squeamish.

CREATURE FEATURES

Common ladybugs

7-spot ladybug
(*Coccinella septempunctata*)
This is the iconic ladybug and the one that gives the family its common name, the seven spots symbolizing Our Lady's seven sorrows. It is native to Europe but found across the globe.

22-spot ladybug
(*Psyllobora vigintiduo-punctata*)
One of several species that do not have red as a background color, the 22-spot is also unusual in that it is not a predator and feeds on mildew (mold). It is native to Europe.

Harlequin ladybug
(*Harmonia axyridis*)
This large species gets its name because it comes in a huge variety of colors and patterns. Originally from Asia, it has spread around the world and earned itself a bad reputation for preying on native ladybug species.

HEAD   ELYTRON

ABDOMEN   LEG   WING

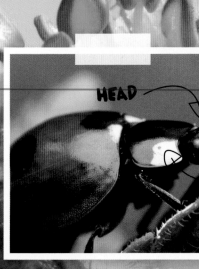

HEAD   EYES   MOUTHPARTS   PRONOTUM

Don't mistake the large white marks at the front for eyes! They are simply colored marks on the pronotum—the front part of the thorax. The actual head of the ladybug is much smaller.

CATCHING YOUR BEAST

In summer you can find ladybugs by searching with your eyes through garden plants such as roses, beans, sweet peas, or even stinging nettles (wear gloves so you don't get stung). Because these beetles are so brightly colored, they stand out and are easy to see. The larvae and pupae can be found the same way.

To find less common species, place a white sheet or umbrella under a bush and shake the leaves. Insects will fall onto the sheet. Transport your ladybugs home in a jar, but keep any larvae you find in separate containers, since they have a tendency to be cannibalistic.

Keep me well stocked with aphids. I eat a lot!

LADYBUG ENCLOSURE

Most ladybugs can be easily kept in simple containers. Any small, transparent container will do. A 4 in (10 cm) wide dish can house up to 15 ladybugs, but I tend to keep 5 per dish—otherwise you'll have to find a lot of food!

1.

Line an empty container with paper towels and stock it with aphids and some vegetation for the ladybugs to climb on.

2.

Transfer the ladybugs to their new home. Use a paintbrush to move them without injuring them. Don't forget to put the lid on afterward!

This ladybug is eating an aphid. Turn the page to see this in more detail!

Dead aphids

Cleaning
Ladybugs are very vulnerable to disease caused by bacteria or fungi, so a daily clean-up to remove dead aphids and other debris is recommended. Ideally, cycle your ladybugs between two containers, cleaning out the used one each time you empty it.

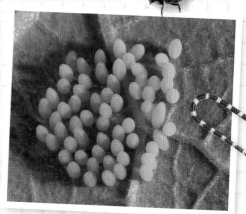

Keep an eye out for eggs. Ladybugs tend to lay their clutches of bowling pin-shaped eggs on the sides of the container. When the young hatch they like to make a first meal of their eggshells. Don't give them aphids until they have walked away from the eggshells.

FEEDING TIME

Ladybugs are predators. The larvae and the adults both prey on aphids—the tiny sap-sucking insects, also called greenflies or blackflies, that infest garden plants. The biggest challenge you'll have as a ladybug farmer will be keeping your beetles supplied with food, and that means you either have to be a dedicated aphid hunter and gatherer or an aphid farmer, too. These weird little unloved but incredibly successful insects are fascinating in their own right, so I've dedicated a section entirely to them (see page 18).

Good places to find aphids are the fresh growing tips or buds of roses, beans, and sweet peas; the undersides of maple and lime tree leaves; thistles; and probably the most reliable—stinging nettles (wear gloves if you handle these). There are two ways of harvesting the aphids. One is to use scissors to snip off a whole stem. The other is to use a paintbrush to knock aphids off one by one.

To harvest aphids with a paintbrush, hold a pot or jar underneath the colony and gently sweep them off.

A pair of ladybugs will need at least 20 aphids a day to keep them in tip-top breeding condition.

Cut a piece of stem that's infested with aphids. Make sure it's small enough to fit inside your ladybug enclosure.

Look for an oily liquid coming out of the pointed "cornicles" on the rear end of aphids when they're under attack. This is a defensive chemical used to ward off ladybugs.

Sweet pea plant

I'm off.

FEEDING TIME

If you were to scale up your ladybug house, it would be like a cage of ferocious tigers that were never satisfied and needed a continuous supply of live victims.

FROM EGG TO EATING MACHINE

If your ladybugs are happy, well fed, and not all ladies (or men), you will possibly get eggs. Some species will lay eggs only during spring or early summer, while others, such as the 7-spot ladybug, breed continuously if they have enough light, warmth, and food. Look after your "baby bugs" well and you can **watch the whole life cycle unfold** before your eyes.

Close-up of a ladybug larva

2. **Once they've eaten** their own eggshells, they begin their marauding lifestyle. At first they're dwarfed by full-grown aphids, but they will climb on top and, while riding piggyback, bite into the aphid and suck its blood—vampire jockeys!

3. **As the larvae** grow, they molt, shedding their skin three times and becoming meaner looking as they get bigger. They behave even more ruthlessly than before and will now start to chew up all of their prey— soft parts, hard parts, legs, antennae, and all.

HELP!!!

5. **The pupa** remains in place while the beetle within takes shape. Then, after a couple of weeks, out pops a ladybug. But it looks unlike any ladybug you've ever seen—has there been a terrible mix-up at the body shop? It's not red and black but a pale, washed-out yellow. And where's that smooth, domed back formed from the glossy wing cases? Instead, this little, damp, crumpled creature staggers out and sits there...

6. **Over the next** few hours, the saggy, baggy wings and wing cases slowly pump up, and the ladybug starts to take shape.

1. **The eggs** are laid in clutches of up to 300. (It's best to separate eggs and adults at this stage so the adults don't eat the eggs.) A week later, they hatch and you get your first look at a "baby bug." These odd little things look like evil caterpillars, and I guess that's what they are.

Chemical weapons

The bright colors of ladybugs make them stand out to our eyes. In nature, animals often use bright colors like these to advertise how poisonous or foul-tasting they are. Ladybugs are no exception—**apparently they taste awful and bitter.**

And that's not the only defensive trick they have up their sleeves...

If harassed by ants, ladybugs clamp their bodies down, hiding their legs under their impenetrable wing cases. The legs tuck neatly into grooves on the underside of the thorax and abdomen, leaving no fragile parts sticking out.

4. **When the larva is** about 2 weeks old, its skin splits for the last time and, just as with caterpillars, a pupa emerges. Attached by the tip of its abdomen to a plant or the container, it sits still unless bothered by a curious poke with a paintbrush, when it will twitch its head end up and down. It is thought this is a defense against parasites and predators.

If the clamp-down fails, ladybugs leak. Yep, they ooze a foul-tasting and foul-smelling liquid—a defensive technique known as "reflex bleeding." If you pick up a ladybug, you'll see the stuff staining your fingers. The liquid oozes out of leg joints and passes along grooves in the body, quickly coating the ladybug in a bitter mixture containing protective chemicals called alkaloids. Despite this, some animals will very happily eat them. Maybe they like their food a little tangy?

Don't prod me too hard!

7. **Next,** the wing cases and pronotum blush and color up (which might take a few days to do completely). When they have dried and hardened, it's time to go on the hunt again for more aphids to victimize.

Ooze

SPIDERS

Spiders are a massive and diverse group of animal, with over **40,000 species**, ranging in size from one that could sit on a pinhead to the massive goliath tarantula, which would have trouble sitting on the palm of an outstretched hand. Despite such variation, they are all instantly recognizable as spiders in that they have a body made up of two main parts (see right) and, of course, those infamous eight legs.

Red-kneed tarantula

Take care
not to grab or harrass unidentified spiders, since some species can give a nasty nip—particularly the North American hobo spider, which looks like a house spider.

SPINNERETS
At the rear of the abdomen are silk glands, or spinnerets, that produce silk for webs. Most spiders have three pairs. At their tips are tiny nozzles called spigots.

Abdomen

Cephalothorax

CREATURE FEATURES

SENSORY HAIRS
Scattered among the hairs are special sensory hairs attached to nerves at their base. These hairs feel vibrations and some can taste.

ABDOMEN
The rearmost of the two main body parts is the abdomen (belly), which contains organs associated with digestion, breathing, breeding, and silk production.

LEGS
All spiders have eight.

CEPHALOTHORAX
In spiders the head is fused with the thorax (chest) to form the cephalothorax (Latin for "head-chest"). This is one of the spider's two main body parts.

Baby house spider

EYES
Spiders usually have six or eight eyes, but poor vision. The size and arrangement of the eyes can help you identify the species.

PALPS
If you think you've counted 10 legs, you've probably counted the palps. These are used for feeling and mating. The tips, which in adult males can look like boxing gloves, are sperm transfer organs designed to fit into the female's body.

FANGS
The fangs (chelicerae) inject deadly venom and digestive juices into prey.

Tegenaria domestica

Pardosa monticola

Pholcus

House spider ✓

The European house spider (*Tegenaria domestica*), which is common across Europe and North America, is easy to keep and makes a great pet. Even better is its larger cousin, the giant house spider (*Tegenaria duellica*). These are the most entertaining, since you get to see all the wonderful details of your animal and its behavior.

Wolf spiders ✓

The free-ranging wolf spiders make the best spider pets. To keep these you need to add a little dirt or potting soil to your spider house, and you could try planting some living plants and adding other "furniture" to make it really interesting for both you and your captive.

Daddy-long-legs ✓

Another spider you're likely to find at home is the daddy-long-legs spider (*Pholcus*), which makes fine, tangled cobwebs high in the corners of our rooms. It makes an interesting pet and is easier to find than *Tegenaria*.

Garden spider ✗

The garden spider is common across the world and catches prey in that classic doily of death, the orb web. But garden spiders need a lot of room to make their webs, so they are not well suited to life in an animal tank.

HOW TO CATCH 'EM

Tegenaria

 Even the most clean house has quiet corners where spiders lurk. Try behind the TV, the couch, in the broom closet, under the stairs, or in the backyard shed. Look for webs and use a pocket flashlight—*Tegenaria* likes to hide in dark recesses.

Tegenaria is tricky to catch. Its sensory hairs make it incredibly sensitive to vibration—just a careless sigh from the spider hunter could send it scuttling into an inconvenient recess. Try and predict its direction of travel and have ready a container with a tight-fitting lid.

Daddy-long-legs are easy to catch. Rather than running away they do a strange little dance, shaking their bodies around so quickly that they become a blur. This makes them difficult to pick up if you're a bird with nothing but a beak, but it's really easy if you have a jam jar!

Use a paintbrush or a pencil to gently poke Tegenaria out of its web or recess. Don't worry about damaging the web—it will make another one for you anyway.

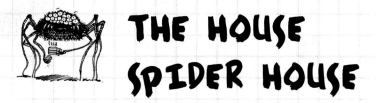

THE HOUSE SPIDER HOUSE

Setting up a house for a house spider (*Tegenaria*) couldn't be easier. I use a plastic animal tank with a tight-fitting lid. If you like, add "furniture" to act as a lair—a piece of bark or broken flowerpot is perfect. Keep the tank away from direct sunlight and add a wad of damp moss. Keep this moist at all times so the spider can drink when it needs to. I also spray with a mist sprayer once a day.

1. Release your captive into its new home and quickly close the lid. Your spider will soon make itself at home, or rather make itself *a* home—within an hour or so you might notice a very light and fine framework of a web.

Old food

2. Over the next few weeks your spider will build up its web until it's created quite a work of art. It might look like a random tangle, but watch how your spider uses it—you'll realize it has order and function. You might have to view your spider at night to see it out and about. Try and identify which parts of the web it waits on, where its lair is, and what it does with its food. It's handy from time to time to remove old prey items or molted skins. This can by tricky, so I like to use long tweezers or chopsticks to pick out the small pieces.

FEEDING

Finding food
Anything a spider can overpower is prey. House spiders normally feed on moths or flies, and you can provide either, but flies are easiest. To harvest them, leave food or compost outside to rot, and sweep up visiting flies in a net. You can also catch flies resting on the wall by placing a jar over them. Then slip paper or cardboard between the jar and wall to trap them.

Dinner time

Release a fly into the tank or, better still, throw it into the web. When the spider feels the web move, it will leap upon its prey and deliver a lethal bite. Watch the fangs in action as the spider injects the venom that paralyzes and starts to digest the body. Spiders can't eat solids, so their victims must be predigested. The resulting juices are sucked up through the mouth and filtered through bristles and hairs—a little like sucking minestrone soup through your teeth and steering clear of the noodles!

STUFF TO LOOK OUT FOR

Molting
If your spider loses its appetite or changes color, it may be about to molt. If you're lucky, you might see the molt take place. The spider's skin lifts off like a cap and a pale new spider bursts out, pulling all eight legs with it—like someone taking off four pairs of pants at once!

Old skin

See what happens if you introduce lots of flies at once. Your spider may rush around collecting as many as possible, paralyzing each one, and then wrapping them in silk to devour later.

GREENBOTTLE FLY

Breeding

If you keep wolf spiders, put a few together and they might breed. The female will carry her egg sac around with her (another use for silk), but after a while the sac will vanish and she'll look oddly hairy. Look closer and you'll see that the "hairs" are a mass of tiny spiderlings. They cling to special, handlelike hairs on the mother's abdomen.

Drinking

Just after you've sprayed your spider tank or refreshed the water dish, watch out for drinking. To do this the animal positions itself over the water source and crouches down, pushing its mouth onto the wet surface. Then, using powerful sucking muscles, it slurps up the liquid.

CRICKETS & KATYDIDS

Crickets, grasshoppers, and katydids often get mixed up. This isn't surprising, since they belong to the same family, look similar, and share the same powerful hind legs that make them such good leapers and so tricky to catch. But while grasshoppers are plant-eaters, crickets and katydids (bush crickets) have more varied diets and some species are ruthless predators, which makes them fascinating to keep in a bug zoo. If you look after them well and keep them warm, they will also entertain you with their songs.

There's no sound coming out of my mouth—it's my wings that are singing!

ANTENNAE
Crickets and katydids have long antennae (feelers) that may be even longer than their bodies.

LEGS
The back pair are modified for jumping. Just below the "knee" (middle joint) of the front leg is a sort of ear used to detect the songs (chirps) of other insects.

Great green bush cricket (Tettigonia viridissima)

ABDOMEN

SPIRACLES
Insects breathe through small holes called spiracles. These are obvious along the abdomen of large crickets and katydids. In some species you can even see the animal "breathing," the muscles in its abdomen squeezing to pump air in and out of the spiracles.

THORAX

HEAD

WINGS

OVIPOSITOR
It's easy to tell males from females, since females possess a vicious-looking, swordlike appendage that sticks out from the abdomen. This is not a stinger, as people often think, but a totally harmless egg-laying tube called an ovipositor.

CERCI
These little sense organs serve as feelers on the back end of the insect. They are very sensitive and are used in testing, tasting, and feeling what is going on behind the animal—a bit like reversing sensors on a car.

CREATURE FEATURES

OCELLI
Simple eyespots, or ocelli, detect light and shade.

COMPOUND EYE
These big, bulbous eyes are clusters of hundreds of tiny eyes (ommatidia) all working together. Katydids, crickets, and grasshoppers all have excellent vision, which is partly why they're so hard to catch!

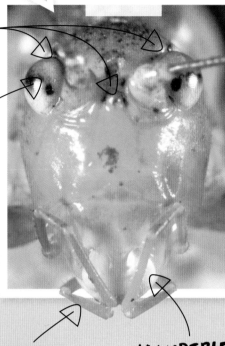

PALPS
These small feelers around the mouth are used to taste food.

MANDIBLES
The powerful, jagged-edged jaws (mandibles) work sideways to mash and tear up food.

WINGS
Most adult crickets and katydids have two pairs of wings. In some species these are used for flight, but in others they are much reduced and serve other purposes. Males use their wings to sing, or "stridulate." They do this by rubbing pegs on one wing against a reinforced vein on the other. Many also hold their wings out a little while singing to form a sounding chamber.

WHO'S WHO?

Grasshoppers are herbivores and are easily recognized by their antennae, which are much shorter and thicker than those of crickets or katydids. They also sing differently, creating sound by rubbing their hind legs against their bodies.

True crickets, which include field crickets and house crickets, live mainly on the ground and eat both animal and plant matter. They have squat, cylindrical bodies and are never green. They are common in the wild in the US and are also sold in pet stores as reptile food.

Katydids live in tall vegetation and range from herbivores to exclusively predatory species. They tend to be nocturnal and well camouflaged, with many being green. They have long, whiplike antennae and are sometimes called long-horned grasshoppers or bush crickets.

Bug hunting
Crickets and katydids announce where they live by singing, but it can be frustrating hunting them when you can hear but not see them! A good technique is to walk through long vegetation keeping your eyes on the area right in front of your feet. It's a technique called "walking them up," and it's used by cranes to hunt insects. Any insects in the grass will spring out as you get near and draw attention to themselves. All you then have to do is grab them and put them in a jar. Another technique is to sweep a large net through long grass, and for some katydids, "bush beating" (see page 24) is the best answer.

KATYDID CRIB

I can watch crickets and katydids for hours—they're always doing something. Katydids in particular love to clamber around in vegetation, so you'll need to provide some form of climbing frame to create a three-dimensional habitat. Plastic animal tanks or large cylindrical containers like the one shown here are good options. These insects have powerful, slicing jaws, so don't rely on netting as a lid—they'll soon shred it and escape!

Making a katydid crib

It's easy to make a katydid or cricket container from a cookie tin. You can also buy specially made versions, but it's cheaper to make one yourself. You'll need a sheet of clear acetate (ask for the stiffest acetate available) from an arts and crafts store or from an office supply store.

Ask an adult to make a few air holes in the lid of the cookie tin. You can use either a drill or a hammer and nail to do this.

Roll the acetate into a cylinder so it fits tightly in the tin. Trim to size and height, but leave a 1 in (2.5 cm) seam. Tape or glue the seam. If you use glue, clamp the seam with clothes pins or bulldog clips while the glue dries. Put the acetate back in the tin, put on the lid, and you're done.

HOME, SWEET HOME

Twigs for your captives to climb on

Tasty treat

Stuff the jar with tissue to stop your critters from falling in and drowning.

Add a container of damp sand for females to lay eggs in.

If you put live cuttings in the container, stand them in a jar of water.

Some katydids are highly predatory, which makes them fun to keep, with feeding time providing a lot of action. You can give them aphids, flies, mealworms, moths, maggots, or any other small creatures. Most crickets and katydids don't just eat flesh—they like a varied diet and will eat a bit of everything, including some fresh greens. A selection of leaves covered with aphids makes a good three-course meal, with a main dish of insect flesh, a little side salad to nibble, and a sweet dessert of honeydew!

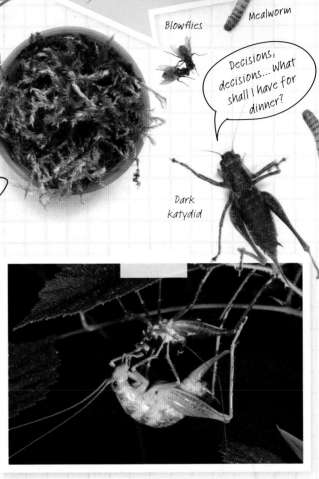

FEEDING TIME

Blowflies

Mealworm

Decisions, decisions... What shall I have for dinner?

Dark katydid

Water can be provided in the standard upturned bottle lid, filled with a wad of wet cotton balls or moss. Spray the moss or cotton daily with warm water.

LOOK FOR

Growing up

Young crickets and katydids are called nymphs. When they molt for the last time and become adults, they acquire their wings, which means they can start to stridulate (sing). This is when the fun begins and you start to see new behavior. You may want to reorganize your set-up at this stage. Try keeping a group of females with one male and watch what happens. Does the male start singing to attract females? Does the song change when females approach him? What happens if you put two adult males in the same territory?

Molting

This is spectacular to see in crickets and katydids because of their unfeasibly long feelers! Watch the old skin split behind the head and the fresh, new insect squeeze itself out, legs, antennae, and all. Look for pieces of white, squiggly string—these are trachea, the breathing tubes of the insect that have been turned inside out. The molting period is a sensitive time: the newly emerged insect is soft and vulnerable (be careful not to disturb it) and runs the risk of being eaten by one of its cannibalistic roommates!

Mating

You'll almost certainly see your insects mating, and you may even see a big white fluffy lump of gloop being produced by the male and carried by the female. This is a bag of sperm called a spermatophore and the female will use it to fertilize her eggs.

Singing

Males do most of the singing, and only when they're warm. It's said you can tell the temperature by timing a cricket's chirps. Why not test the theory? Count how many chirps come from a single insect in 15 seconds. Do this a few times and figure out the average. Divide this number by two and add six. In theory, the answer should be the temperature in degrees Celsius! (You can then convert to Fahrenheit if you like.) Does it work?

Gosh, it's hot! Doh, ray, me, fa, so, lah....

Laying

Katydids lay their eggs on leaves but crickets lay them in the ground. If you set out a pot of sand, you may be able to watch female crickets laying eggs in it. It's a fascinating thing to watch. If you want to see the eggs, provide damp cotton balls instead of sand and look through them with a magnifying glass.

÷2 +6

PSEUDOSCORPIONS

These mite-munching murderers can be found anywhere and everywhere, but we seldom see them on account of their tiny size. Called pseudoscorpions, which means "false scorpions," they are every bit as spectacular as their MUCH bigger cousins. And I emphasize the word "much" because these animals are smaller than small—a big one is a mere ¼ in (6 mm) long, and the biggest species in the world reaches only ½ in (12 mm).

Pseudoscorpions are members of a class of animals known as ARACHNIDS, which also includes spiders and true scorpions. Like all arachnids, pseudoscorpions have four pairs of walking legs. If you get to ogle one up close, you'll also see how they got their name: the front end looks just like a scorpion, with a pair of mean-looking pincers. It's at the other end that things look totally and obviously different—pseudoscorpions don't have a stinger in their tail because they don't even have a tail! But they are **ruthless little predators** nonetheless and pack a small punch, delivering poison to their prey through the tips of the pincers. The bug zookeeper doesn't need to worry about this, since the venom is delivered in such tiny quantities that it is effective only against the pseudoscorpion's equally minuscule prey.

CREATURE FEATURES

LEGS
Being an arachnid, the pseudoscorpion has legs arranged in four pairs—that's eight in total.

To get the best out of these tiny creatures and really impress your pals, use a USB microscope to see them in their full neat and nippy glory.

ACTUAL SIZE!

PINCERS

More correctly called pedipalps, the pincers are held out when the scorpion is moving, since they are covered in long sensory hairs that help the animal feel its way around. The venom gland is located in the mobile half of each claw (the "finger").

ABDOMEN

The rear part of the body is called the abdomen (or opisthoma) and is a fairly dumpy, rounded, pear-shaped thing. It contains all the essential organs and so is protected, segment by segment, by little armored plates made of a hard stuff called chitin. These plates are called tergites (on the top) and sternites (underneath).

CEPHALOTHORAX

It's that word again—the "head chest," a fusion of the head, with all its sensory organs, and the thorax, the motor room containing all the muscles used to operate the legs.

EYES

Pseudoscorpions don't have very good eyes, and some don't have any at all, relying instead on the sensory hairs on their bodies to tell them about their environment and prey. Most have either two or four simple, domed eyes on either side of the head.

CHELICERAE

On each side of the mouth are the pseudoscorpion's evil-looking jaws, called chelicerae. These look a little like scissors and work like them, too, slicing up and butchering prey. The chelicerae also have silk glands, which, rather surprisingly, these animals use to weave platforms and cushions used in mating and molting.

Finding them...
a needle in a haystack springs to mind!

The easy way
Pseudoscorpions are everywhere. They live in compost heaps, piles of dead leaves ("leaf litter"), moss, under stones, in your house... The problem is their size and color, which make them a challenge to spot. One cunning way to catch them is to make what's known as a **Tullgren funnel**, where a bright light is used to drive them into a jar. The principle at work here is that creatures that live in leaf litter tend to flee from light and head toward nice dark places with high humidity, where they don't have to face their deadliest enemy: dehydration.

The hard way
Another technique is to scoop up a bucket of leaf litter, spread it out on a white sheet or tray, and then go through it by hand until you find your catch. It's when pseudoscorpions move that you're most likely to pick them out from among the similarly colored litter. Their glossy appearance also helps. I found the little beast on these pages by accident when I was looking for snails under some old bricks at the bottom of my yard.

MAKING A TULLGREN FUNNEL

1. **Pack leaf litter** into a plastic funnel and wedge it in a jar, having put some damp tissue in the jar. Set a lamp over the leaves, taking care not to let the bulb flashlight the leaves or make them hot. (You don't want to burn the house down—the words "looking for pseudoscorpions" won't work on the insurance report!)

2. **Leave the lamp** on overnight. The next day, investigate the contents of your jar. You'll probably have an odd assortment of leaf-litter creatures such as mites, earwigs, springtails, and other stuff, but with a bit of luck you'll have a few pseudoscorpions, too!

slug

How do pseudoscorpions get into your house?

Microhabitat

Because pseudoscorpions are so very tiny, you don't need a very big habitat. In fact, the biggest problem with keeping these creatures is keeping track of them. All they need to do is hunker down in the groove of a leaf and you've lost them! So I cannot stress this enough: try and make their containers as small as possible.

Catch me if you can!

PSEUDOSCORPION ENCLOSURE

Furnish the habitat with the sort of material you found your animal living in, such as bits of dead leaves. To keep the humidity up, include a pad of living moss.

An empty glitter tube makes a good home for pseudoscorpions.

Keep an eye out for runaways!

Some people have trouble keeping pseudoscorpions alive for more than a few days. The secret seems to be maintaining humidity and plentiful food. One trick to control humidity is to put plaster of Paris in the floor of the container, let it set, and then moisten it before you build your habitat.

Mini-meals

Since your tiny predators feed on even tinier prey in the wild, you will have the tricky task of supplying them with a regular supply of leaf-litter creatures, or at least a regular supply of leaf litter. Not much is known about what pseudoscorpions really like to eat, but a selection of live food including springtails and soil mites should keep your captives happy.

Springtail

Use a soft paintbrush to pick up your pseudoscorpion.

They cling to flies and hitch a ride!

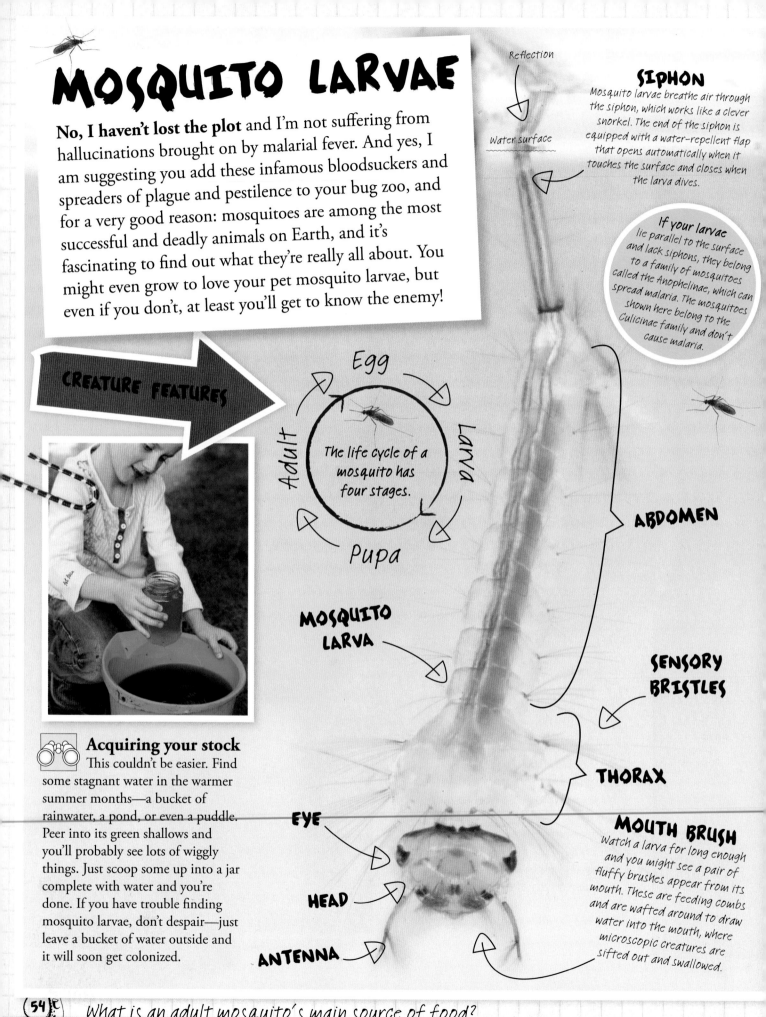

MOSQUITO LARVAE

No, I haven't lost the plot and I'm not suffering from hallucinations brought on by malarial fever. And yes, I am suggesting you add these infamous bloodsuckers and spreaders of plague and pestilence to your bug zoo, and for a very good reason: mosquitoes are among the most successful and deadly animals on Earth, and it's fascinating to find out what they're really all about. You might even grow to love your pet mosquito larvae, but even if you don't, at least you'll get to know the enemy!

CREATURE FEATURES

Acquiring your stock
This couldn't be easier. Find some stagnant water in the warmer summer months—a bucket of rainwater, a pond, or even a puddle. Peer into its green shallows and you'll probably see lots of wiggly things. Just scoop some up into a jar complete with water and you're done. If you have trouble finding mosquito larvae, don't despair—just leave a bucket of water outside and it will soon get colonized.

Reflection

Water surface

SIPHON
Mosquito larvae breathe air through the siphon, which works like a clever snorkel. The end of the siphon is equipped with a water-repellent flap that opens automatically when it touches the surface and closes when the larva dives.

If your larvae lie parallel to the surface and lack siphons, they belong to a family of mosquitoes called the Anophelinae, which can spread malaria. The mosquitoes shown here belong to the Culicinae family and don't cause malaria.

Egg

Larva

Adult

The life cycle of a mosquito has four stages.

Pupa

MOSQUITO LARVA

ABDOMEN

SENSORY BRISTLES

THORAX

EYE

HEAD

ANTENNA

MOUTH BRUSH
Watch a larva for long enough and you might see a pair of fluffy brushes appear from its mouth. These are feeding combs and are wafted around to draw water into the mouth, where microscopic creatures are sifted out and swallowed.

What is an adult mosquito's main source of food?

Mosquito larvae need very little space—a tiny pot or jar will do. Their ability to thrive in tiny puddles of water is what makes mosquitoes so successful and also such a nuisance. In countries where malaria spread by mosquitoes is a big problem, people have tried getting rid of the disease by removing pools of stagnant water. The pest controllers were mystified when this didn't work, until they discovered why: old car tires trap puddles of rainwater, and the mosquitoes were happily breeding away in them.

Stagnant green water →

Molted skins
As your little larvae grow they will molt and old skins will float to the surface. Mosquito larvae have four "instars" (larval stages), each bigger than the last.

← Molted skin

Larva ("wriggler") →

Pupa ("tumbler") →

Feeding
You might think that feeding such small animals would be fiddly, especially when you learn that they eat microscopic organisms like algae. How do you sort all that out? Fortunately it couldn't be easier. All that stuff is what makes stagnant water green, so all you need do is spoon stagnant green water into your micro-aquarium. For the mosquito larvae, it's like living in their own pea soup, only it's got no peas in it!

It's one of the few times that stagnant water in an aquarium is a good thing!

Tumblers
When larvae are fully grown, they turn into pupae that look like strange little shrimp. This is the resting stage in the life cycle, but you wouldn't think it when you see how active they are—just jogging the jar is enough to send them twitching down into the water, only to bob back up again. This behavior has earned them the name "tumblers." Instead of breathing through a siphon, the tumblers use "breathing trumpets" on the head. They swim by flicking a paddle on the tail.

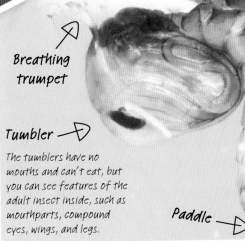

Breathing trumpet →

Tumbler →

Reflection →

The tumblers have no mouths and can't eat, but you can see features of the adult insect inside, such as mouthparts, compound eyes, wings, and legs.

Paddle →

Taking flight
After about four days, the tumbler's skin splits and out pops a mosquito. The mosquito hangs around on the surface film to dry out and then takes off. I know what you're thinking: release these bloodsuckers and they'll come back and bite you. Well, assuming you've got *Culex pipiens* (the most common species and the one on these pages), you have little to worry about: it feeds on birds rather than humans!

Nectar: Female mosquitoes drink blood only when they're about to make eggs.

55

DRAGONFLY LARVAE

The word dragonfly conjures up images of needles of bright color zinging and zooming over a pond in the summer sun. Unfortunately, this high-energy lifestyle makes dragonflies impossible to keep in your bug zoo as adults—they'd smash themselves to pieces. However, they spend most of their lives underwater as larvae, and these "baby dragons" are not only easy to keep but are also every bit as exciting as their parents. Care for them well and they'll eventually reward you with one of the most breathtaking spectacles of the natural world.

PREY GRABBERS

Look close at a dragonfly larva's face and you'll see what looks like a vicious pair of jaws. This is the tip of the larva's "mask"—an extensible feeding device that unfolds to reach out and grab prey. See how it works on page 59.

CREATURE FEATURES

EYES
Huge, googly compound eyes either side of the head give these insects excellent vision.

ANTENNAE

MASK
Under the head is a hinged arm ending in powerful claws for snatching prey.

WING BUDS
On top of the animal (not visible here) are four wing buds that get bigger as the larva grows. These will eventually become the gauzy, sparkling wings of an adult dragonfly, but for now they double as supplementary gills.

THORAX

LEGS (6)
These are equipped with grappling hooks for gripping water plants.

ABDOMEN
This consists of 10 segments and contains all the breathing, breeding, and digestive parts.

Dragonfly skin

Keeping dragonfly larvae in your zoo is like keeping miniature crocodiles. Just like crocs, they are sly, skulking predators that hunt by lying in wait and then ambushing anything that moves. Just imagine what it would be like to scale one of these things up to the size of a 16-foot (5-meter) croc!

Land a larva

Use a fishing net (or kitchen strainer attached to a stick) to drag up lots of weeds and mud from the bottom of a pond. Tip the contents of the net into a large white tray or a similar container and then, using a teaspoon, gently sort through it to look for dragonfly larvae. You'll need to concentrate: the larvae are well camouflaged and some are even covered in downy hair, making them hard to see unless they make a small movement and blow their cover!

Transfer each larva to an individual pot of water. It's important to keep them separate since they'll very happily eat each other if crowded together, and don't collect more than two or three. Return the rest of the pond life to the pond when you've finished.

You might find damselfly larvae in your sample of pond life. These look like dragonfly larvae but are more delicate, with three "tails" that are actually gills and are often flattened and leaflike in shape. Damselfly larvae can be kept in the same way as dragonflies and make a great addition to your bug zoo.

FRESHWATER AQUARIUM

A small plastic or glass aquarium is ideal for dragonfly larvae. The idea is to re-create the natural environment the larvae live in and to make it varied, so the larvae can choose where they want to be. To keep the water fresh, you will need to do at least a partial water change every week or so and remove debris such as leftover meals from the water.

1.

Put washed gravel or sand in the bottom of the tank. Gently slope the gravel so that it will make a nice backdrop and any debris will collect at the front, where it's easy to scoop out.

2.

Add pondweed, stones, and any other aquarium decorations. Heap the gravel over the roots of the plants or fix them into small pots first to keep them in place.

Damselfly skin

3.

Put newspaper over the gravel (so the water won't mess it up) and gently pour in rainwater or tap water that's been left to stand for a few days.

4.

Leave the aquarium for at least a day to settle and clear. Position it somewhere light but not in direct sunlight.

A tea strainer makes a handy tool for moving larvae.

THE DRAGON'S DEN

Feeding time in the dragon's den is a truly exciting time and one of the highlights of your bug zoo. Once you put live prey in the tank, it won't be long before some serious predation is underway. You can even tease your dragonfly into striking with its mask by holding prey in front of it with homemade wooden tweezers.

Some dragonfly larvae can extend and withdraw their masks to capture prey in less than 15 milliseconds. That's faster than the human eye can register!

Feeding
Dragonfly larvae need a constant supply of fresh—and that means living—food. Anything that will wriggle and move in the water will catch your larva's huge eyes, but you'll need to experiment to see what size prey it wants to tackle. Small larvae might prefer tiny prey such as water fleas or mosquito larvae. For bigger ones, bloodworms (common in ponds), earthworms, and fish fry are tackled with gusto.

FEEDING TIME

Larva coming in for the kill

Mealworm

Tweezers

You can tease your larva into striking by dangling wriggling prey near it or even by shining a light spot with an LED flashlight. To hold the prey, use chopsticks or make wooden tweezers from kebab sticks. To make the tweezers, wrap a rubber band around one stick to form a pivot and another rubber band around the "handles" to make the long ends springy.

Collecting exuviae

You might be alarmed one day to find what looks like a dead larva on the surface of the water in your tank. More often than not this is just the empty skin, or "exuviae," left behind when a dragonfly or damselfly larva molts—something that happens many times as they grow up. Look in the water and you'll find a bigger larva (perhaps 25 percent bigger) looking a little pale and vulnerable as he waits for his new skin to harden up. The empty skins can be collected and dried. Try sticking them on a piece of cardboard with the dates of the molts and you'll get a nice little growth chart of your pet's progress.

WATER TO WINGS

Place sticks in the tank so the larva can climb out for its final molt.

Feeding mask

Hinge

The breathtaking finale of your larva's life is its transformation into an adult dragonfly or damselfly. It's a true miracle and something everyone should see at least once in their life. Predicting it can be difficult, but there are clues. The larva's wing buds will flesh out and its eyes will look vacant. It will lose its appetite and start to hang around the surface as its gills stop working. Make sure there are sticks that it can climb up to leave the water. When the time comes, the larva will climb one of these, hunch up, and its skin will split open. Very slowly, a ghostly pale and very crumpled dragonfly will almost ooze out. It's moments like this that digital cameras were made for! Watch the wings inflate and the body color up and harden. Finally, it will beat its sparkling wings and take off.

If your exuviae is dry and crispy, soak it in water to make it flexible again. Then use a pin to pull out the mask. This is a great way of getting to know your larva without causing the living animal any stress.

It's time to say goodbye and open a door or window to let your captive fly free!

Once my wings have dried I'll be off!

I'm outta here!

BACKSWIMMERS

The backswimmer is a ferocious underwater predator found in ponds, lakes, and streams. It reminds me in some ways of a bird of prey, but instead of surveying the land from high above, it hangs upside down from the water surface to watch the watery world below. And when it spots victims with its huge eyes, it swoops down and plucks them from the pondweed before returning to its perch to devour them. Its active lifestyle makes this bug-eyed monster a very entertaining addition to your zoo.

Don't get bitten by the bug!
Backswimmers are also known as water wasps and water bees because if handled roughly they will use their stabbing mouthparts in self-defense, and their bite hurts. They won't bite if they are supported on a hand, but don't squeeze them!

CREATURE FEATURES

Water surface

Reflection of backswimmer

FRONT LEGS
The first two pairs of legs are tipped with claws for grasping prey.

All this hanging around has given me a headache!

REAR LEGS
The rear legs are fringed with fine hairs and are used like oars to row the insect through the water.

ROSTRUM OR BEAK
This is a sharp and flexible feeding tube used to stab prey and inject a toxic saliva, which subdues and digests the victim. The rostrum is then used like a drinking straw to suck up the victim's body fluids.

HEAD

COMPOUND EYES
The enormous compound eyes, each made of hundreds of tiny eyes, look like mean wraparound shades or a sci-fi space helmet. Like the eyes of dragonflies, which are similar, they form very good images and are used to locate prey. They are also sensitive to polarized light (more about that later).

Built like a boat

The backswimmer not only has "oars" for propelling itself but also has a body shaped like the hull of a rowboat—perfect for slipping easily through the water. Because it swims upside down on its back, it was given its name of "backswimmer."

THORAX

ABDOMEN

WAXY HAIRS

A layer of waxy, water-repellent hairs covers the abdomen. Backswimmers trap a film of air under the hair and around the body.

AIR BUBBLE

Although backswimmers live in water, they breathe air. They trap a silvery film of air around the body and under the wings, enclosing themselves in a kind of bubble. They use this bubble to breathe and to control their buoyancy.

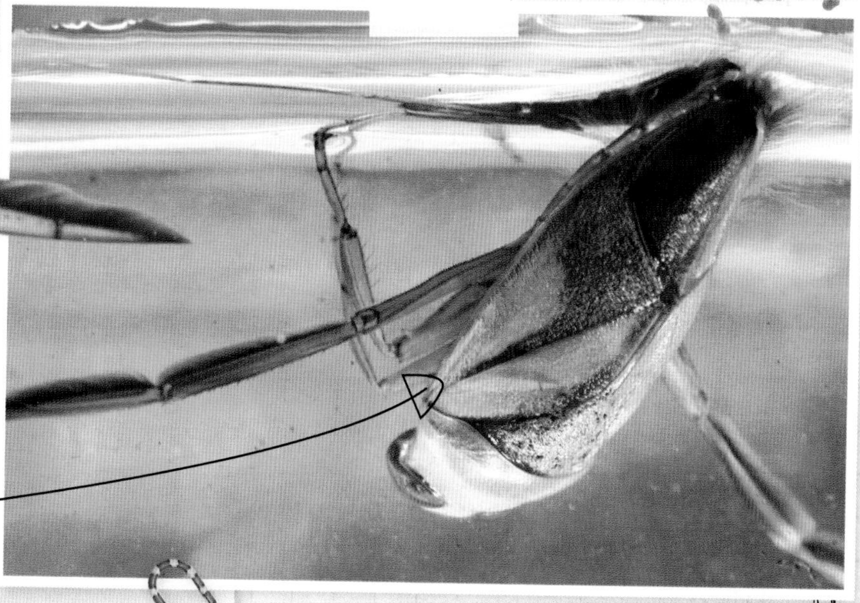

AIR HOLE

When the tip of the abdomen touches the water surface, the waxy hairs around it spread out and an air hole opens up. This allows the insect to replenish its air supply. The hairs close over the hole automatically when the animal dives.

WINGS

It might surprise you to learn that backswimmers can fly! Their flight wings are protected under leathery wing cases. Air trapped under them gives the wings a silvery appearance in water.

THE POOLHOUSE

Mealworm

Backswimmers need a freshwater home made in the same way as the dragonfly aquarium on page 57. They don't need a huge tank—a large jar or fish bowl will do. Since they are carnivorous, it's not a good idea to crowd them, keep youngsters with adults, or put other creatures with them (except for live prey). A big jar like the one below will comfortably house 2–3 adults.

🔭 Finding them

Pond, lakes, and slow-moving streams are good places to look. Approach slowly and look carefully—they will appear to be hanging from the surface. Even if they dive down, disturbed by your approach, they will bob back up. Use a net or a strainer on a stick to scoop them out. Be quick and have a bucket or tray of water on standby for your captives, since they will immediately start hopping and jumping around to try and escape.

Lesser backswimmer

Close relatives

Backswimmers make up a family of insects known as Notonectidae. You might also come across smaller but similar-looking insects called water boatmen (family Corixidae), which swim the right way up and stay near the bottom, where they feed on plants. Although not as big and spectacular as notonectids, they are very cool and even sing to each other, making a rasping noise by rubbing their legs on their heads!

Don't forget!
Backswimmers can fly—your container will need a lid or some netting held in place with a rubber band or string.

BACKSWIMMER CONTAINER

Pond weed

Rock

Rainwater or pond water

Washed sand or gravel

Feeding

Backswimmers only take live and wriggling prey. Mine eat everything from small worms and mealworms (available in pet stores) to fly maggots (from fishing stores), flies, and tadpoles. You can also put small pond creatures in with them, since this is what they'd eat in the wild. As soon as the prey is in the water, watch the hunt. Besides using their eyes to see prey, backswimmers have sensory hairs on their legs and abdomens that allow them to feel the movements of live prey and so capture them in dark or murky water.

Worm

When they attack prey, you will be able to watch the grisly feeding process in detail. First, the backswimmer stabs its victim with its highly mobile and flexible beak. Then, when the prey is paralyzed or dead, you'll see the killer start sucking out the body fluids. I've watched one devour a tadpole this way, the tadpole's body slowly deflating like a balloon over an hour or so.

THINGS TO LOOK FOR

Sunny side up

You can demonstrate exactly what it is that makes a backswimmer swim upside down by putting one in a clear container of water and, in a dark room, lighting the insect from below with a flashlight—it will flip up the right way around!

Grooming time
Like many predators from peregrine falcons to your pet cat, backswimmers are fastidious in their vanity. They will spend a lot of time grooming, rubbing their eyes, wings, and waterproof hair with their legs.

Backswimmer becomes aeronaut

Backswimmers are often the first creatures to colonize a new pond—but how? Well, you can see for yourself. Taking care not to get bitten, remove one from the water, hold it in the palm of your hand and let it dry out. This may take a few minutes, and they do have a tendency to flip around to try and hop back into the water—so be prepared to juggle it.

After a while, when the insect realizes it's not going to flip itself back into the water, it will give up this tactic and fall back on another mode of locomotion. Watch it carefully as it wipes its eyes and back with its legs—this is the backswimmer's preflight check. Soon after it will "unclip" its wings and spread them before suddenly springing into the air and buzzing off!

Yes, they are excellent flyers and once they're up in the air will search for a new pond, river, or lake by looking for the polarized light that these natural surfaces reflect. The problem is that glass buildings and car windshields also reflect polarized light, which means that backswimmers can make mistakes. Sit in a parking lot on a hot and sunny day and you'll sometimes see backswimmers and other pond insects such as water beetles come crashing down!

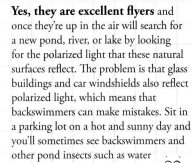

INDEX

Yum, dinner!

Acknowledgments and picture credits

Nick Baker would like to thank James at absolute data services for loan of the Dino-lite microscope, and Andy at Alana Ecology.

Dorling Kindersley would like to thank Scarlet Heap and Stanley Heap for appearing in photographs, and Ceri Baker for her lovely lunches on photoshoots.

The publisher would also like to thank the following for their kind permission to reproduce their photographs.

(Key: a-above; b-below/bottom; c-centre; f-far; l-left; r-right; t-top)

Alamy Images: Arco Images GmbH / H. Frei 56tl; Lee Beel 27bc; Blickwinkel / Hecker 33bc; Blickwinkel / Kottmann 53bc;

Blickwinkel / MeulvanCauteren 32clb; Nigel Cattlin 21ca; Matt Cole 11tr; Graphic Science 21clb, 35tr; David J. Green - animals 13ca; Chris Howes / Wild Places 49fclb; Hazel Jeffs 59bc; Lars S. Madsen 62fclb; Mercer / Insects 56; Nature Picture Library / Jose B. Ruiz 44bc; Robert Pickett / Papilio 11cra; Stefan Sollfors 43tc; Barry Turner 36bl; WildPictures 18tl. **Ardea:** Johan de Meester 25fcr; Steve Hopkin 36clb, 41fcra; David Spears (Last Refuge) 10br. **Corbis:** Naturfoto Honal / Klaus Honal 59fbr, 59fcr, 59fcra, 59fcrb, 59ftr; Hans Pfletschinger / Science Faction 41cl; Fritz Rauschenbach 47cla; Stefan Sollfors / Science Faction 45bc, 45clb; Visuals Unlimited 21cb, 29tr, 47ftr; Stuart Westmorland 14cl. **Dorling Kindersley:** Natural History Museum, London 6cl, 22fclb; Oxford Scientific Films 37br, 41ftl; Jerry Young 6crb, 11ftl. **Flickr.**

com: Michael Balke 29crb; Rodents Rule / Carron Brown 17fcra; Captain Spaulding78 / Tim 11tc. **FLPA:** Nigel Cattlin 11cr, 11crb; Imagebroker 46-47; Imagebroker / Andre Skonieczny, I 36r; Mitsuhiko Imamori / Minden Pictures 10tr; Roger Tidman 47fcra. **Getty Images:** Botanica / Steve Satushek 19tl; Flickr / Achim Mittler, Frankfurt am Main 36bc, 40cr; National Geographic / Wolcott Henry 10clb; Panoramic Images 43ftr; Photographer's Choice / Derek Croucher 36cl; Photographer's Choice / Guy Edwardes 27cb; Photographer's Choice / Sami Sarkis 63crb; Photolibrary / Colin Milkins 20b; Photolibrary / Oxford Scientific 41tc; Stock Image / Stephen Swain Photography 16tl; Stone / Peter J. Bryant / BPS 22-23cb; Stone / NHMPL 21cla; Workbook Stock / Steve Satushek 47cr. **Krister Hall:** Photo.net 11br. **iStockphoto.com:** Alexander Hafemann 4 (blank page); Tomasz

Kopalski 17crb; Alexander Kuzovlev 7fcra (snail), 15bl, 64tr; Dave Lewis 17cr, 17ftr; Trevor Nielson 11bl (35mm frame), 17ca (35mm frame); Bill Noll 53ftr; Tomasz Zachariasz 11fcr, 12tr. **Thomas Marent:** 6-7t (butterfly), 26bl, 26cl, 26fbl, 26fcl, 26tc, 27br, 27cla; naturepl.com: Philippe Clement 29cra. **Photolibrary:** Oxford Scientific (OSF) 28crb; Oxford Scientific (OSF) / David M Dennis 49cr. **Photoshot:** NHPA / A.N.T. Photo Library 49fbl; NHPA / George Bernard 55crb; NHPA / Laurie Campbell 10fclb. **Science Photo Library:** Dr. Jeremy Burgess 40cl; Claude Nuridsany & Marie Perennou 40bl, 40br, 41bl; Andrew Syred 40ftl.

All other images © Dorling Kindersley
For further information see: www.dkimages.com